The Benefits and Costs
of the Kyoto Protocol

The Benefits and Costs
of the Kyoto Protocol

Jason Shogren

The AEI Press

Publisher for the American Enterprise Institute

WASHINGTON, D.C.

1999

This essay draws on work with Michael Toman forthcoming in "Climate Change Policy," in Public Policies for Environmental Protection, *2d ed., edited by Paul Portney and Robert Stavins (Washington, D.C.: Resources for the Future). All views herein are mine. I wish to thank Joseph Aldy, Robert Hahn, Sally Kane, Randall Lutter, David Montgomery, Al McGartland, Ray Squitieri, Robert Stavins, Robert Tuccillo, Jonathan Weiner, and participants at the AEI conference on Climate Change Policy for their helpful comments.*

Distributed to the Trade by National Book Network, 15200 NBN Way, Blue Ridge Summit, PA 17214. To order call toll free 1-800-462-6420 or 1-717-794-3800. For all other inquiries please contact the AEI Press, 1150 Seventeenth Street, N.W., Washington, D.C. 20036 or call 1-800-862-5801.

ISBN 0-8447-7134-1

1 3 5 7 9 10 8 6 4 2

The AEI Press
Publisher for the American Enterprise Institute
1150 17th Street, N.W.
Washington, D.C. 20036

Contents

Foreword

This volume is one in a series commissioned by the American Enterprise Institute to contribute to the debates over global environmental policy issues. Until very recently, American environmental policy was directed toward problems that were seen to be of a purely, or at least largely, domestic nature. Decisions concerning emissions standards for automobiles and power plants, for example, were set with reference to their effect on the quality of air Americans breathe.

That is no longer the case. Policymakers increasingly find that debates over environmental standards have become globalized, to borrow a word that has come into fashion in several contexts. Global warming is the most prominent of those issues: Americans now confront claims that the types of cars they choose to drive, the amount and mix of energy they consume in their homes and factories, and the organization of their basic industries all have a direct effect on the lives of citizens of other countries—and, in some formulations, may affect the future of the planet itself.

Other issues range from the management of forests, fisheries, and water resources to the preservation of species and the search for new energy sources. Not far in the background of all those new debates, however, are the oldest subjects of international politics—competition for resources and competing interests and ideas concerning economic growth, the distribution of wealth, and the terms of trade.

An important consequence of those developments is that the arenas in which environmental policy is determined are increasingly international—not just debates in the U.S. Congress, rulemaking proceedings at the Environmental Protection Agency, and implementation decisions by the states and municipalities, but opaque diplomatic "frameworks" and "protocols" hammered out in remote locales. To some, that constitutes a dangerous surrender of national sovereignty; to others, it heralds a new era of American cooperation with other nations that is propelled by the realities of an interdependent world. To policymakers themselves, it means that familiar questions of the benefits and costs of environmental rules are now enmeshed with questions of sovereignty and political legitimacy, of the possibility of large international income transfers, and of the relations of developed to developing countries.

In short, environmental issues are becoming as much a question of foreign policy as of domestic policy; indeed, the Clinton administration has made what it calls "environmental diplomacy" a centerpiece of this country's foreign policy.

AEI's project on global environmental policy includes contributions from scholars in many academic disciplines and features frequent lectures and seminars at the Institute's headquarters as well as this series of studies. We hope that the project will illuminate the many complex issues confronting those attempting to strike a balance between environmental quality and the other goals of industrialized and emerging economies.

CHRISTOPHER DEMUTH
ROBERT W. HAHN
American Enterprise Institute
for Public Policy Research

1

Introduction

SEBASTIAN: What a strange drowsiness possesses them!
ANTONIO: It is the quality o' the climate.
—Shakespeare, *The Tempest*, Act 2, Scene 1

Some experts in the rules of civilized engagement view the 1997 Kyoto accord on the reduction of carbon emissions as a crucial first step in addressing climate change; others see the accord as a serious misstep; few see it as the answer. The protocol's short-term comeback to a long-term question has left most reviewers demanding either deeper emission reductions or broader emission coverage or both. The complexities and frustrations are manifest in the comment from Bert Bolin, former chair of the Intergovernmental Panel on Climate Change:

> The Kyoto conference did not achieve much with regard to limiting the buildup of greenhouse gases in the atmosphere. . . . Only if the new cooperation among countries succeeds will the Kyoto conference represent a step toward the ultimate objective of the convention.[1]

But regardless of one's view, the 1997 Kyoto accord did signal a new earnestness of intent toward addressing the perceived risk of climate change. The Kyoto accord demands that developed nations turn their economies so as to hit differentiated, sub–1990 level carbon emission targets within the next decade or so. Meanwhile, developing nations sit on the sideline uncommitted, serious in their refusal to stifle economic growth by controlling their swelling emissions.

The Kyoto protocol asks for immediate action to address an uncertain, long-term, global threat in which the nations soon to be the world's largest emitters may never participate. Think of trying to turn a battleship on a dime with a third of the crew on-board: improbable but doable. But for what benefit and at what cost?

This essay examines the benefits and costs of the Kyoto protocol. I take the Kyoto protocol at face value, consider what the accord asks for and allows, and evaluate the potential benefits and costs that might accrue if the accord enters into force in 1999. My attempt to remain dispassionate occasionally wavers—a remnant from lively White House discussions past while I served as the senior economist for environmental policy at the Council of Economic Advisers during the run-up to Kyoto. The negotiating pressure at that time made me appreciate the force of an observation Dales made in 1968:

> The politicians must decide what the public wants and stake their political lives on their decision; they are in a much better position to assess the benefits and costs of their action (or inaction) than any body of experts.[2]

Still, economists are not shy about saying that behavior matters more to climate policy than many people think; that wealth spent on climate policy cannot be spent somewhere else; and that more reasonable policy makes it possible to provide more human and environmental health with less wealth. Thus, assessing benefits and costs can help frame the climate change debate by identifying the elements of the Kyoto accord that inflate costs with no additional benefits.[3] I begin by considering what the literature says about estimating the benefits and costs of compliance for the United States and the world and then examine the key modeling assumptions that drive those estimates—for example, the stringency of the abatement policy, the flexibility of policy instruments such as international emission-trading systems or sinks, and the development and diffusion of technology.

Not surprisingly, the benefits and costs of the Kyoto accord depend on what we choose to believe about the nature of climate protection. Most economists believe that the threat of catastrophe will have to be imminent for the Kyoto protocol to make sense, given the likely impact of compliance on the U.S. economy.

2

The Kyoto Protocol

What madman would be against a goal of achieving more financial and commercial well-being while preventing untold global catastrophe? Essentially that was what the representatives of some 150 countries supposedly set out to do when they met in Kyoto, Japan, in December 1997 at the Third Conference of the Parties to the United Nations Framework Convention on Climate Change. Their task was to create a legally binding international agreement for climate protection—the so-called Kyoto protocol. The protocol will enter into force ninety days after the date on which

> not less than 55 Parties to the Convention, incorporating Parties included in Annex I which accounted in total for at least 55 per cent of the total carbon dioxide emissions for 1990 of the Parties included in Annex I, have deposited their instruments of ratification, acceptance, approval or accession (Article 24).

The protocol was open for signatures by parties between March 16, 1998, and March 15, 1999. In November 1998 the United States was the sixtieth nation to sign, although the Senate has not ratified the agreement, and ratification—not signatures—is what matters.

The Kyoto conference culminated years of negotiations to strengthen the first international climate change treaty signed by over 160 countries at the 1992 Earth Summit in Rio de Janeiro. The original treaty, the Framework on Climate Change, called on industrial nations voluntarily to reduce their greenhouse gas emissions to 1990 levels by 2000 (see table 2-1). Emissions from most nations, however, have actually risen since that treaty. Because voluntary actions did not do the job, many advocates of climate protection saw the Kyoto protocol as the way to correct that perceived misdirection.

The Kyoto protocol takes a "deep, then broad" stand. "Deep" in that the emission targets require what many observers consider a rapid reduction in carbon emissions for industrial nations; "then broad" in that developing nations currently have no obligations but are hoped to join the agreement eventually once someone convinces them that it is in their best interest to join. The "deep, then broad" angle has left many experts unimpressed by the protocol, which seems to some a quick political fix rather than a serious response driven by the natural sciences and economics.[4]

Provisions of the Protocol

Targets and Timetables (Article 3). The protocol set a legally binding target for thirty-nine of the world's most developed countries to reduce greenhouse gas emissions in aggregate by 5.2 percent from a 1990 baseline for the period 2008–2012. The targets are differentiated by nation and range from an 8 percent reduction (the European Union) to a 10 percent increase (Iceland) from 1990 levels. The United States agreed to a target of 7 percent reduction; Japan a 6 percent reduction (see table 2-2). Each party must show demonstrable progress toward meeting its target by 2005.

Nations' Joint Actions to Hit Their Target (Article 4). The protocol lets a group of nations form a multicountry "bubble" in which the group has an overall target to reach. Each nation inside the bubble has its own commitment to the rest of the group. The bubble was designed to meet the demand

Table 2-1

Total Carbon Dioxide Emissions of Annex I Parties in 1990 for the Purposes of Article 25 of the Kyoto Protocol

Party	Emissions (gigagrams)	Percentage
Australia	288,965	2.1
Austria	59,200	.4
Belgium	113,405	.8
Bulgaria	82,990	.6
Canada	457,441	3.3
Czech Republic	169,514	1.2
Denmark	52,100	.4
Estonia	37,797	.3
Finland	53,900	.4
France	366,536	2.7
Germany	1,012,443	7.4
Greece	82,100	.6
Hungary	71,673	.5
Iceland	2,172	.0
Ireland	30,719	.2
Italy	428,941	3.1
Japan	1,173,360	8.5
Latvia	22,976	.2
Liechtenstein	208	.0
Luxembourg	11,343	.1
Monaco	71	.0
Netherlands	167,600	1.2
New Zealand	25,530	.2
Norway	35,533	.3
Poland	414,930	3.0
Portugal	42,148	.3
Romania	171,103	1.2
Russian Federation	2,388,720	17.4
Slovakia	58,278	.4
Spain	260,654	1.9
Sweden	61,256	.4
Switzerland	43,600	.3
United Kingdom of Great Britain and Northern Ireland	584,078	4.3
United States of America	4,957,022	36.1
Total	13,728,306	100.0

Note: Data are based on the information from the thirty-four Annex I parties that submitted their first national communications on or before December 11, 1997, as compiled by the secretariat in several documents (A/AC.237/81; FCCC/CP/1996/12/Add.2 and FCCC/SB/1997/6). Some of the communications included data on CO_2 emissions by sources and removals by sinks from land-use change and forestry, but since different ways of reporting were used, those data are not included.

Source: Report of the Conference of the Parties on Its Third Session, Held at Kyoto from 1 to 11 December 1997 (FCCC/CP/1997/7/Add.1. 18 March 1998).

Table 2-2

Annex B

Party	Quantified Emission Limitation or Reduction Commitment (percentage of base year or period)
Australia	108
Austria	92
Belgium	92
Bulgaria[a]	92
Canada	94
Croatia[a]	95
Czech Republic[a]	92
Denmark	92
Estonia[a]	92
European Community	92
Finland	92
France	92
Germany	92
Greece	92
Hungary[a]	94
Iceland	110
Ireland	92
Italy	92
Japan	94
Latvia[a]	92
Liechtenstein	92
Lithuania[a]	92
Luxembourg	92
Monaco	92
Netherlands	92
New Zealand	100
Norway	101
Poland[a]	94
Portugal	92
Romania[a]	92
Russian Federation[a]	100
Slovakia[a]	92
Slovenia[a]	92
Spain	92
Sweden	92
Switzerland	92
Ukraine[a]	100
United Kingdom of Great Britain and Northern Ireland	92
United States of America	93

a. This country is undergoing the process of transition to a market economy.

of the European Union that it be able to comply as a group. The bubble requires the EU to adjust its commitment if its membership enlarges.

Greenhouse Gases (Article 3-Annex A). The protocol covers six greenhouse gases—carbon dioxide, methane, nitrous oxide, hydrofluorocarbons, perfluorocarbons, and sulfur hexafluoride—as a "basket." The last three use a 1995 baseline instead of 1990. The inclusion of the six gases allows for some flexibility in reaching the target. Reductions in one gas can be used to substitute for reductions in other gases.

Emission Trading (Article 17). The protocol allows for emission trading among the nations to fulfill their commitments. An emission-trading program provides greater flexibility to a nation to achieve its target. The domestic government can issue "greenhouse gas emission permits" to the private sector that equal the target set by the protocol. While the permits could then be freely bought and sold domestically between firms (Article 2), it is left unclear as to whether firms can trade across borders. The trading price forces sources to reduce greenhouse gas emissions so long as the tax exceeded the incremental cost of emissions reduction. That would stimulate fossil-fuel users to improve energy efficiency, use less carbon-intensive fuels, and consume less of the goods and services produced in the carbon-intensive ways. Apparently, disagreements about international trading were almost enough to deflate the conference. In return for emission trading, the United States gave up its opposition to the EU bubble.

Joint Implementation and the Clean Development Mechanism (Articles 6 and 12). Joint implementation refers to one nation's getting credit for implementing a project to reduce carbon emissions in another country. Joint implementation is limited to the parties. A new device, the clean development mechanism, was designed for joint projects with developing nations through the payment of a special administrative fee by developed nations. According to the protocol,

> [t]he purpose of the clean development mechanism shall be to assist Parties not included in Annex I in achieving sustainable development and in contributing to the ultimate objective of the Convention, and to assist Parties included in Annex I in achieving compliance with their quantified emission limitation and reduction commitments under Article 3.

A small portion of proceeds from the special fee is to be used to help the poorest of the poor nations, such as the island states, adapt to climate change.

Carbon Sinks (Article 3). The protocol allows for carbon sinks—land and forestry practices that remove carbon emissions from the atmosphere. Sinks could play an important role for some nations because they represent a low-cost option. Sinks are ambiguously defined in the protocol and will be a challenge to measure.[5] Sinks might even turn out to be an escape valve for the United States since little is known with certainty about the net uptake of the terrestrial sinks in North America. According to the State Department, once we adjust the U.S. accounting method, sinks will account for about 3 percent of the 7 percent reduction below 1990 levels that the accord requires.[6]

No Harmonization of Actions. The protocol allows each nation to figure out its own best strategy to meet its commitment. Not everyone sees that as a good thing. Some critics have argued that the world would have been better served by a common action rather than a common target.[7]

Omissions from the Protocol

Developing-Country Participation. No agreement was reached in Kyoto on what commitment developing countries should assume to reduce their greenhouse gas emissions. And the protocol does not include a separate article for nations to assume binding targets voluntarily. But it is clear to everyone that climate protection requires the participation of the developing countries because by the middle of the next century, they are predicted to generate the largest share of carbon emissions. But those nations remain unmoved by the protocol. They have no incentive to reduce their economic growth. China, for example, is the second largest emitter after the United States, but its per capita emissions are about one-seventh of those in the United States. A Chinese delegate captured the sentiment underlying the opposition: "What they [developed nations] are doing is luxury emissions; what we are doing is survival emissions."[8] Substantial compensation might be required to induce developing nations' necessary participation.

Specifics on Emission Trading and the Clean Development Mechanism. The protocol also left the specific rules and regulations about international emissions trading to be defined at a future date. Although both trading and the mechanism have the potential to generate low-cost emissions reductions for developed countries and tangible benefits to the host country, two factors limit their scope—transaction costs and additionality. Transaction costs are the time, effort, and other resources needed to search out, negotiate, consummate, and secure governmental approvals for heterogeneous deals. How the rules are eventually defined will determine the friction in all those flexibility tools. Additionality reflects the fear that people will try to use the clean development mechanism to get credit for emissions changes that would have happened despite some reduction project. Options to address additionality range from detailed scrutiny of every project before approval to the development of simple formulas applied across all projects. An obvious trade-off exists between reliability and cost among those options. The developers of the mechanism need to define and pretest the institutional, administrative, and financial arrangements, the guidelines on the criteria for eligibility and certification, and verification and monitoring of emission reductions.

Specifics on Compliance and Enforcement. Both emission trading and the clean development mechanism require measures to assess compliance and to hold participants responsible for noncompliance. Under the framework convention and the Kyoto protocol, the Annex I–capped countries are ultimately responsible for achieving their emissions targets, whether they are net buyers or sellers of permits or credits. Presumably the protocol parties will then reassign that responsibility to the domestic private sector through strategies to monitor emissions and spot check specific investment projects. The protocol says that enforcement procedures to deal with noncompliance will be established at the first meeting of the parties to the protocol. But until the details are fleshed out and that uncertainty is resolved, those firms falling under a trading system will remain skeptical about the workability of the scheme. For instance, whether the buyer or seller should be liable for the penalty of trading a permit that should not have been traded remains a major question.

3

Benefits from the Kyoto Protocol

The potential benefits from the protocol are captured by the avoided damages from climate change.[9] Potential climate risks avoided include more severe weather patterns, hobbled ecosystems, less biodiversity, less potable water, loss of coastal areas from rising sea levels, rises in mean temperature, and the increased incidence of infectious diseases such as malaria, yellow fever, and cholera. On the plus side, climate change might benefit agriculture and forestry by increasing productivity with longer growing seasons and more fertilization. Those gains (or losses) can be categorized into four broad sets, increasingly difficult to quantify—the avoided losses to market goods and services, nonmarket goods, secondary impacts, and catastrophes.

Traditionally, people have judged the benefits of climate protection as the reduction in human and environmental risks from the business-as-usual baseline. Under that baseline, modelers have estimated that carbon concentrations might be expected to double preindustrial levels within the next half century, with mean temperatures predicted to rise by about 1 degree Celsius by 2050 and by 2.5 degrees by 2100. With the Kyoto protocol, the expected rate of slowing temperature rise is minor—between 4 and 14 percent of the business-as-usual baseline, with global mean-warming reductions between .04 and .10 degree Celsius by 2050 and .08 to .28 degree Celsius by 2100.[10]

Researchers have estimated that the total impact on gross world product from not complying with the climate change protocol is about 1 or 2 percent annually. The impact on gross domestic product in the United States has been estimated to be around plus or minus 1 percent annually. Most industries in the developed nations are not affected by climate—less than 3 percent of U.S. livelihoods, for instance, are earned in agriculture and other climate-sensitive outdoor activities.[11] And even if we include the potential nonmarket damages, Nordhaus has argued that the market and nonmarket benefits to the United States are probably at most about 2 percent of GDP.[12] At the margin, the damages avoided have been estimated to be about $25 per ton of carbon, the extra benefit obtained from reducing carbon emissions by one ton.[13] Those impacts are not trivial, but the impact on economic output is not likely to cause the next global depression either.

Schelling views climate protection as a political problem whose costs will be relatively low: "a few trillion dollars over the next 30 or 40 years, out of an OECD GDP rising from $15 trillion to $30–$40 trillion annually."[14] Although doable, he wonders whether that is really the right consideration. He points out that climate policy really amounts to a wealth transfer from today's industrial nations to the future generations in the developing nations. The benefits from the Kyoto protocol are most likely to accrue to the future generations in developing nations because their economies depend more on favorable climate for agriculture, forestry, and fishing. He wonders whether it would be better to invest in development today than to pay for climate relief tomorrow.

Two topics in nonmarket valuation are likely to trigger major debates about the likely magnitude of potential benefits—human health and ecosystem–endangered species services. First, consider health. Some assert that the potential threats to human health include old scourges like cholera, plague, yellow and dengue fever, tuberculosis, malaria, and thirty diseases new to medicine, like E. coli, hantavirus, and HIV.[15] Less is said about the odds that the events will come to pass. What are the odds, what is the variability around those odds, and how credible are they?[16]

Despite the warnings, the cause and effects are still uncertain. It is not clear that malaria rates will increase, because mosquitoes may fail to adapt to changes in temperature, humidity, or precipitation.[17] And attached to those threats must be advances in technology, nutrition, and medical care. Adaptation may be the key to prevention. Once we acknowledge that adaptation plays a key role, we must account for the fact that risk depends on private and collective choices. The economic variables that drive adaptation, such as relative price and wealth, must be considered when estimating health risk. Given the relative marginal effectiveness of different self-protection actions, how people confront risk differs across individuals and situations, even though the natural phenomena that trigger those actions apply equally to everyone.

More information is needed to determine the bias in assessing health risks solely in terms of natural science information, given that the sources of systematic variation are relative prices, incomes, and other economic and social parameters. If economists are going to be effective in the debate over setting health-based standards, they must insert themselves into the econometrics of epidemiology.[18] Biases associated with measurement and specification errors are prevalent. When account is taken of self-protection behaviors, ambient concentrations are not synonymous with exposure. Economic variables affect behavior, which affects the risks faced by people, and exclusion of those variables from risk assessment biases predictions. Studies have shown that people persistently below the poverty line are far more likely to become sick than wealthy people for a variety of reasons including habits, lifestyle, less medical screening, and the ability to self-protect. The evidence suggests that behavioral choices frequently associated with poverty (for example, high discount rates) are the most significant threat to health. Wealth equals health, even in warmer or colder climates.

Estimating the social value of endangered species and ecosystem services is also a challenge. When considering endangered species values, people disagree about the usefulness of the primary tool to reveal the monetary value of those preferences—contingent valuation surveys. Such public opinion surveys use a sequence of questions to put a monetary value on personal preferences. But since people are responding to a survey instead of facing their own budget constraint and actually spending their own money, no market discipline exists to challenge their statements. For instance, if we summed the stated preferences from various endangered species surveys as a crude measure of benefits, the average person was willing to pay about $1,000 to protect eighteen different species. Multiplying $1,000 by the number of U.S. households suggests that we would be willing to pay over 1 percent of GDP to preserve less than 2 percent of the endangered species.[19] Many will find those values to be suspiciously high. Despite the challenge in measuring the value of preservation, determining a plausible range for those values is needed for helpful judgments about the potential for climate change benefits.

We might claim that climate protection might avoid damages to the global ecosystem services in the range of $33 trillion.[20] That estimate is meaningless, however, since willingness to pay is constrained by the world's ability to pay—a world GDP of about $18 trillion.[21] And if we account for the fact that all people make some contribution to total world income, the potential maximum ecosystem benefits are easily cut in half.[22] But it is questionable whether those numbers really mean anything at all, given the false baseline of an all-or-nothing outcome with climate change. The most likely changes will not be a binomial Armageddon versus Eden revelation.

Another way to amplify the benefits of the Kyoto protocol is to consider the potential secondary impacts that come from discouraging coal and other fossil-fuel consumption. The Kyoto protocol would reduce emissions of such air pollutants as carbon monoxide, sulfur and nitrogen oxides, and toxic trace pollutants in exhaust gases. By reducing BTUs generated by fossil-fuel consumption, emissions of those pollutants would inevitably fall and reduce damages to health, visibility, materials, and crops. Studies in Europe and the United States have estimated that the nonclimate benefits might be as large as or larger than the benefits from avoiding climate change. The estimated secondary benefits range from $3 to $78 per ton of carbon reduction (in 1992 dollars) based on a pre-1997 ozone/particulate matter National Ambient Air Quality Standards (NAAQS) baseline.[23] The benefits from reducing air pollution damages could offset 30 to 100 percent of carbon abatement costs, given the pre-NAAQS baseline.

But should those secondary impacts count when considering the level of climate protection? One argument against their inclusion is the fear of double counting. The already existing NAAQS rules that were tightened in 1997, but subsequently overturned by a federal appeals court, rather than climate change policy, might produce the majority of the potential health benefits. The Clinton administration has estimated that extra benefits from climate change, given a post-NAAQS baseline, will be about $1 billion in 2010.[24] If our current air quality policies are effective, they should be capturing all the positive net social benefits. Claiming those net benefits for climate change just says that our other environmental policies are flawed and that we should be focusing attention on improving them. Climate change policy should not serve as a catch-all bailout for all our perceived social ills.

Finally, researchers, policymakers, and politicians have raised the specter of catastrophe and surprise. Modelers often presume that climate change will be gradual—a slow and steady rise in temperature or precipitation. But many people warn that the assumption of a steady flow ignores the real risk of a catastrophe such as a structural change in ocean currents like the Gulf Stream, the melting of the Western Antarctic ice sheet, or waves of environmental refugees.

Those threats are enough to scare most people into action. While careful not to make any causal link, some point to El Niño as an illustrative example of the damages we might expect with climate change. Stuart Eizenstat, under secretary of state for economic, business, and agricultural affairs, said, "For a preview of the type of severe weather . . . look at the devastation wrought by this winter's El Niño."[25] But according to the Federal Emergency Management Agency, the cost of the El Niño winter in the United States did not significantly differ from that of the previous two winters— $289 million in 1997–1998 compared with $294 million in 1996–1997 and $280 million in 1995–1996.[26]

The problem is that researchers do not have any reasonable estimates of the odds that such events will come to pass. The best those researchers are willing to say is that such severe events are "uncertain."[27] But all "all severity–no probability" scenarios can lead people to automatic, predictable reactions. The challenge is to get researchers to quantify those odds for more informed policy judgments. It matters whether the odds are 10 percent or one-tenth of .1 percent.

In addition, the business-as-usual baseline is not the only benchmark to judge the benefits of the Kyoto protocol. In fact, the business-as-usual path is less credible after the Kyoto accord because the developed world has already agreed to do something to address climate change.[28] According to Article 2 of the Framework Convention on Climate Change, the objective is to stabilize "greenhouse gas concentrations in the atmosphere at a level that would prevent dangerous anthropogenic interference with the climate system." Numerous different emissions-reduction scenarios can work to stabilize concentrations at some level, including the "broad, then deep" pathway recommended by many researchers and policymakers: broad participation by both developed and developing countries and a gradual emission-reduction path to achieve a desired long-term concentration target.[29]

Delay is not denial, some say.[30] The "broad, then deep" recommendation represents the view that we can allow emissions to grow at least for the next few decades before serious reductions are necessary.[31] While advocates of that policy run the risk of being dubbed irrelevant to the process, the moderate-reduction baseline calls for an emission path that peaks around 2020 and would result in essentially the same concentration level in 2100 as the Kyoto protocol specified—at a fraction of the costs. Implementation of that benchmark would require an initial, modest increase in the price of carbon emissions and a credible commitment to increase the price over time. Shifting emissions reductions into the future allows time for a gradual adaptation of the energy capital stock by developing low-cost and low-carbon-technology substitutes that remove carbon from the atmosphere via the carbon cycle. Because the economy yields a positive return on capital, future reductions can be made with a smaller commitment of today's resources.

The benefits generated by that moderate benchmark are nearly identical to those produced by the Kyoto protocol, even accounting for secondary and catastrophic impacts. The temperature difference between the Kyoto protocol and the moderate baseline are less than .1 degree Celsius at any time over the next century. That small difference reflects the long lags in emission flows and concentration stocks over the century and the fact that the most serious emissions will come later in the century from the expanding economies of the developing nations. The net result is that the Kyoto protocol did not gain any benefits over the next-best alternative.

4

The Costs of the Kyoto Protocol

Estimates of the costs of the Kyoto protocol vary markedly. Some studies suggest that the United States could meet its target at negligible or modest cost; others call the protocol an "economic disarmament" driven by rank political opportunism. To assume that the costs are somewhere in between puts the theorist at risk of being compared to a cigarette manufacturer who robs children of life or to a fool who has bestowed long-lasting economic advantages on his international competitors.

On the modest side is the Clinton administration's report on the Kyoto protocol that the Council of Economic Advisers produced. Again relative to the business-as-usual baseline, that report states that the costs to the United States to meet its Kyoto target are "likely to be modest if those reductions are undertaken in an efficient manner employing the flexibility measures of emissions trading (both domestic and international), joint implementation, and the Clean Development Mechanism." By "modest" the administration means an annual GDP drop of less than .5 percent—roughly some $10 billion dollars; no expected negative effect on the trade deficit; gasoline prices increased by about five cents a gallon; lower electricity rates; and no "significant aggregate employment effect."[32] The marginal costs in that case are about $10 to $20 per ton of carbon. Essentially, the administration's estimates of costs use a "broad, then deep" baseline. And those estimates might be plausible if all goes exactly right with the world—a big "if."

In contrast, forecasts from two economic consulting firms, WEFA Inc. and DRI/McGraw Hill Inc., estimate that the U.S. GDP could decline by nearly 3 percent annually—$250 billion a year—with intranation emission trading. According to those firms, the trade deficit would increase by tens of billions of dollars, gasoline prices would increase by nearly fifty cents a gallon, electricity prices would nearly double, and two million U.S. jobs would disappear.[33] The impact on energy use is analogous to that felt during the decade of OPEC price shocks. The marginal costs are upward of $200 to $300 per ton of carbon. Those analyses find the assumptions of rapid technological improvement problematic and demontrate the likely friction that institutions eventually seeing the light of day would impose on any emission trading or technology transfer system.

Other analysts conclude that the Kyoto protocol will neither destroy national economies nor be costless.[34] Researchers at Resources for the Future, for instance, estimate that Kyoto could cost about 1 percent of GDP annually or in the worst case 2 percent.[35] Energy costs would increase for an average U.S. household by about 25 percent—including a gasoline price rise of thirty cents a gallon—for a total of $2,500 per year. Those estimates fall within the range of Charles River Associates' cost estimates of about 1.4 to 2 percent losses in 2020.[36] The Australian government estimated global losses at about 1 percent annually globally at 2020.[37] Before the Kyoto protocol, the Energy Modeling Forum estimated that the short-term costs of reducing emissions to the 1990 level by 2010 would reduce U.S. GDP by .5 to 1.5 percent annually and that the medium-term costs would decrease GDP by .6 to 2.6 percent by the year 2020.[38] The Energy Modeling Forum has yet to release its estimates since the Kyoto protocol was adopted.

Another interesting story emerges when we compare the costs of the Kyoto accord with the more moderate "broad, then deep" emission path baseline. Nordhaus and Boyer have used the RICE-98 model to address the relative benefits and costs of the Kyoto protocol to a moderate or "optimal" baseline.[39] While preliminary, their results suggest that while both paths yield nearly identical emission reductions, the Kyoto accord without global trading could be eight to fourteen times more expensive than the moderate path. In general and for all models, cost estimates are likely to be on the low side for several reasons. First, models assume the most efficient possible climate control program although today only one such program is continuing. Second, models assume that the control program is announced early and maintained indefinitely, although a government will be hard pressed to maintain consistent control over the decades. In addition, many models focus on long-term equilibrium and ignore the short-run adjustments such as the oil shocks of the 1970s. We have good reasons to believe that any international or domestic emission-trading program or clean development mechanism will have significant transaction costs stemming from market friction. Some economists think that those costs would raise cost estimates by a factor of one to four. That would cause the Kyoto protocol to reduce GDP by 1 to 10 percent from the baseline. For comparison, the United States now spends about 2 percent of GDP on all environmental programs combined.[40]

Finally, the facts do not support the common assertion that modelers habitually overestimate the costs of environmental regulations so that the estimated costs of complying with the Kyoto accord are excessive. Although economists predicted that the control costs for sulfur dioxide could be $1,500 per ton and today the cost is $100, good reasons exist for that disparity: unanticipated technological breakthroughs, railroad deregulation, and the issue of free permits. Ray Squitieri of the Department of Treasury compiled the actual evidence. He found that cost estimates are just as often on the low side. For instance, predictions straddle actual costs for asbestos, coke ovens, and vinyl chloride regulation; numerous unpredicted changes in technology and the economy occurred to lower the cost of controlling chlorofluorocarbons, cotton dust, and SO_2 emissions. Although the National Ambient Air Quality Standards were estimated to be achieved by 1977, seventy-five areas with a combined population of seventy-five million people have still not attained those standards.

5

What We Choose to Believe about Benefits and Costs of the Protocol

How we see the benefits and costs of the Kyoto accord depends on what we choose to believe about the nature of three elements that underlie climate protection—the cusp of catastrophe, the degree of flexibility, and the origins of technological advance.[41]

The Cusp of Catastrophe

What we choose to believe about the benefits of the Kyoto protocol depends on how we perceive the risk of catastrophe. If we believe that disaster is imminent, emission reductions cannot come soon or fast enough. If we do not believe that disaster is imminent, it is hard to justify the likely costs of the Kyoto protocol without global trading. Reliable information is needed to guide people from their diffuse views about the likelihood of catastrophe. Whether that information will be forthcoming between now and potential ratification fights is unclear.

Numerous unanswered questions persist about the structure of atmospheric systems and their potential thresholds. As Schelling and many others note, uncertainties abound. We do not know which regions will get warmer or cooler; which will get wetter or drier; which will get stormier or calmer. Climate policy debates eventually reach the point in which the modeler is asked whether he has accounted for the likelihood that a change in the ecosystem will be discontinuous—a catastrophe. Most modelers acknowledge that their models do not address the potential for discontinuous shocks, such as a sudden shift in the Gulf Stream or an unraveling of the web of life resulting from the loss of some keystone species.

Some observers view the increased temperature over the past century as well within the bounds of natural variability. Others such as Vice President Gore have asserted that the evidence of global warming keeps "piling up, month after month, week after week. How long is it going to take before these people in Congress get the message?"[42] John Holdren, a member of the president's scientific advisory committee, agrees: "Every day the evidence becomes more persuasive that global warming is underway." But the high variability of daily weather and seasonal means makes discerning trends a challenge; it is difficult to separate signals from natural noise.

That does not necessarily mean that society is on the cusp of catastrophe. The doomsayers have a bad track record. In addition, numerous risk perception studies have revealed that people commonly overestimate the chance that they will suffer from a low probability–high severity event, for example, a nuclear power accident.[43] When the outcome is potentially very bad, people inflate the chance that the outcome will be realized. Policymakers are not immune to that human fallibility. Overestimation of risk can multiply throughout the general public. For example, people pondering the storage of nuclear waste can transform images of a fortified storage facility containing sanitized, air-tight receptacles into an abandoned dump site teeming with rusty, leaking vats of toxic material. The images induce vivid perceptions and cause considerable disagreement about how to regulate the risk.

Experience tells people little about low-probability risks such as climate change. They must rely on outside sources of information to judge the likelihood that a bad event will actually come to pass. And if that outside information stresses severity without giving some notion of the odds, people systematically bias their risk perceptions upward. Other evidence suggests that when people are given good news with the bad, the bad news often dominates.[44]

Of course, sticking one's head in the sand is not particularly useful either. Climate protection is viewed as hedging against uncertainty—planet insurance.[45] As such, it is important that we understand the range of potential impacts, not just the expected value.[46] Peck and Teisberg explore how risks of large losses affect the estimated costs of given climate protection strategies.[47] Using Nordhaus's survey of expert opinions about the odds of losses,[48] those analysts create eight states of nature by assigning either a high or low value to three key parameters that reflect uncertainty—the probability of a loss, the climate sensitivity, and the utility discount rate. The results suggest that the optimal policy under uncertainty is about the same as the policy for the lowest-loss state of nature. That results in part because the lowest-loss state receives the greatest likelihood of coming to pass. A probabilistic damage function based on the mean relative pessimism from the same expert opinion survey suggests that under the extreme damage scenario opined by natural scientists, climate protection is six times more stringent than Nordhaus's original prediction.[49] Using the same opinion survey as the starting point, a third integrated model constructs an empirical relationship between carbon emission accumulation and the odds of a catastrophe.[50] More carbon emissions without a disaster in one year lead to a greater chance of a catastrophe in the next year. The results suggest that the odds that a catastrophe will occur by about 2100 range from 4 to 63 percent, depending on how emissions affect the odds of a loss. While that range does not significantly reduce our uncertainty about the odds of disaster, the framework is a worthy one deserving more attention in future modeling efforts. Commissioning a newer, updated expert opinion survey seems most worthwhile, given the lessons learned over the past decade about the workings of the climate system.

Finally, uncertainty about the underlying physical processes and random variability requires policymakers to decide whether to control for potential catastrophe now or to wait for more information about the climate. The Kyoto protocol reduces emissions and slows learning because less information now exists about the cause and effect. An integrated assessment model with endogenous learning shows that uncertainties about the climate system are resolved in 90 to 160 years, far longer than most people expect.[51] A trade-off exists between emission policy and learning—the more emission reductions, the less learning about the system under study. Policies of climate protection based on a presumption of complete information can be off by as much as 25 percent in either direction once we account for learning. Elements of truth exist on both sides of the debate. Policymakers would serve a more useful role as arbiters who help reconcile risk perceptions rather than inflame the differences. People with a sane expectation of rationality should demand no less.

The Degree of Flexibility

What we choose to believe about the costs of the Kyoto accord can be framed by focusing on whether and how we think the flexibility provisions will come to pass, what we assume about future policy regimes, and how many nations will actually be included in any exchange system. The costs to meet a policy depend on a firm's legal ability to use low-cost carbon reductions and on how quickly society wants to change the energy systems and capital structure of the U.S. economy. A stringent, inflexible carbon policy will induce greater economic burden than a loose, flexible policy. Obviously, more flexibility and more trading partners can reduce costs, as a firm can search out the lowest-cost alternative. We can expect the opposite with inflexible rules and few trading partners. It is estimated that any agreement without the cost flexibility provided by trading will at least double U.S. costs.

We can measure flexibility as the ability to reduce carbon at the lowest cost, either domestically or internationally, including so-called when-and-where flexibility—which assumes that a world emissions budget could be spent optimally over space and time to capture all potential intra- and intertemporal efficiencies. That would allow the banking and borrowing of allowable carbon emissions. Providing a firm or nation more flexibility to reach a given target and timetable also will reduce costs. Almost all studies of the costs of the Kyoto protocol already assume that carbon reductions are implemented domestically with well-designed, cost-effective policy tools like a carbon tax or a system of tradable permits. International flexibility is also key for U.S. firms to meet domestic targets at lower cost by financing the upgrading of inefficient energy facilities in developing countries. Limiting such opportunities for flexibility because of poor policy design, inherent problems in administering international policies, or lack of interest on the part of other countries will mean potentially much higher costs. The key is to distribute emissions internationally so as to minimize the costs of climate policy.

The Kyoto protocol established a narrow coalition of developed nations that now must reach out to the developing countries to join later. That approach begins with a narrow participation by a limited set of nations in a relatively ambitious agreement that involves considerable costs and hence requires fairly sophisticated policy instruments. People have to judge the odds that developing nations will eventually join the protocol. The most contentious issue in Kyoto was how to encourage or pressure developing nations to commit to emission reductions. The United States pushed for a voluntary system, but the European Union maintained that discussions on developing countries should only begin after the developed nations took the lead. China, Brazil, and other nations stopped several efforts in Kyoto to create a voluntary opt-in process for the developing nations to adopt binding commitments. China also successfully opposed putting the issue on the agenda for the convention in Buenos Aires. The difference in outlook is obvious. The developing nations are looking into the future and seeing the other side of the environmental Kuznets curve; the developed nations are looking at today and seeing the steep climb up the same curve. Rich nations got rich through carbon. Poor nations want the same opportunity. Who can blame them? The Kyoto accord runs the risk that the developing countries will never join later because the costs of doing so will be excessive. By increasing the relative costs of carbon in the narrow coalition, carbon-intensive industries will be tempted to move to developing countries, thereby making those economies even more carbon-dependent as they try to grow their way past the real health problems they face now.[52] Their addiction to carbon-based growth increases the costs of joining the treaty. The suppliers of carbon-intensive energy will look for existing markets and will create new markets. If developing countries do not alter their emissions path, global emissions levels will continue to increase even if all the developed nations completely eliminate all their emissions. Without China or India and the rest of the developing world, the Kyoto protocol will not work. The Clinton administration indicated that it would not submit the protocol to the Senate until the developing countries offered evidence of "meaningful participation." Unskilled as I am in affairs of state, my guess is that the debate over whether climate change policy is really backdoor foreign aid will stall serious proposals to pay for meaningful participation over the next decade.

Second, we need to work through the details of how the system would be designed before we can usefully evaluate alternative policies.[53] The Kyoto protocol does not have a set position as to what either a domestic or international trading system would look like. That is serious since we would essentially be creating a new global currency—the "carbo." The global economy would be under the thumb of the institution that controlled the supply of the carbo. Would we give control over to a quasi-independent institution like the Federal Reserve? Would we turn over the carbo supply to Alan

Greenspan? Society would want to turn over the supply to someone who understands how to keep the economy from stagnating, which is not likely to be the administrator of a federal environmental ministry.

What is curious about carbon emissions trading is that its biggest supporters have often been environmental activists rather than economists. The environmental community prefers emissions trading over carbon taxes because the quantity of carbon flowing into the atmosphere is fixed, thereby shifting risk from the environment to the economy in the form of price uncertainty. Some advocates have pushed for relatively high transaction costs that would limit the cost savings of a trading system; others have argued for a flexible system that allows for the banking and borrowing of permits. But many economists have questioned the feasibility of carbon trading because the international market is likely to be thin as most nations have indicated inaudible interest in the system, and the costs of monitoring and enforcing the system are likely to be high.

Defining the rules for flexibile incentive systems is open for development. One way to explore the nature of trading is to test alternative systems in laboratory markets before actual field implementation.[54] Experimental economists could play an important role in reducing the associated uncertainty for both joint implementation and the clean development mechanism. A test carbon emission–trading system designed in laboratory markets could evaluate the institutional factors that will influence the effectiveness of carbon trading. Experimentalists could consider how flexibility in trading, imperfect information, multigas trading, links between domestic and international trading, and other factors will affect the potential efficiency of trading.

A serious effort is vital to understand what aspects of emission trading can reduce the costs of climate change policy. The effort should first design and parameterize a market that reflects the costs and productivity of the countries or regions expected to participate in an emission-trading initiative as suggested in the Kyoto protocol. Researchers could then use the parameters of the nations to design World Wide Web market experiments, to test various trading proposals that have been described to meet the Kyoto protocol objectives by using the market parameterization, to evaluate the robustness of emission-trading market institutions to market "frictions"—impediments to efficient, cost-minimizing market outcomes—and to evaluate how the scope of the market affects market performance.

Third, carbon sinks are a wild card in the search for flexible, low-cost solutions. Recall that a carbon sink is a process that destroys or absorbs greenhouse gases, such as the absorption of atmospheric carbon dioxide by terrestrial and oceanic biota. The main anthropogenic sink is tree planting and other forest management actions. Soils and other types of vegetation also provide a potential sink. Researchers estimate that forests around the world contain about 830 billion metric tons of carbon in their vegetation and soil, with about 1.5 times as much in soil as in vegetation. For the United States, forests are an important terrestrial sink, given that they cover about 750 million acres. Land-use changes in the United States have increased the uptake of carbon to an estimated 200 million metric tons.

A few studies have found that carbon sequestration through sinks could cost as little as $25 per ton in the United States for 150 million metric tons.[55] But serious uncertainties remain about how to measure and account for estimates of net carbon. For example, how forest management activities affect soil carbon is unknown, and since forest soils contain over 50 percent of the total stored forest carbon in the United States, that difference can have a significant impact on estimates. Some researchers have shown that sinks are not so effective as predicted when we account for the interaction of forest reserves and the timber market. The more land that is set aside for carbon sinks, the quicker the cycle of harvesting on other forest land and the less total net carbon sequestration.[56] Some fear that the ambiguities about sinks could divert attention from first-order priorities to second-order technicalities.[57]

Fourth, preexisting distortions created by the existing tax system for labor and capital income amplify the costs of climate protection. Labor and capital taxes distort behavior because they reduce employment and investment levels below what they would have been otherwise. Adding a carbon tax (or permit) that discourages consumption and production further reduces employment and investment, which then exacerbates the labor and capital tax distortions. One estimate is that the amplified distortion will inflate the control costs by some 400 percent.[58] We could reduce those extra costs by channeling the revenue from the carbon tax, if any existed, to reduce the labor and capital taxes and thereby reduce the preexisting distortions. Revenue recycling could shave control costs to 75 percent. But the political reality is that the odds of a tax or permit system that raises revenues to be recycled are unlikely. Carbon permits most likely would be given away for free to producers because of the disastrous BTU tax experience.

Fifth, costs will increase if proposals further restrict flexibility by requiring that nations make some fixed percentage of emissions cuts at home. The EU environmental ministers met after the Kyoto meetings to define a strategy to restrict U.S. efforts to use emission trading to reduce the costs of hitting the target. Seeing trading as flight from responsibility, the EU drafted text for the next negotiations to prevent "loopholes" in the protocol. Although no consensus was reached, some ministers argued that 50 percent of emission reductions must come from domestic cuts. Peter Jorgensen, spokesman for the EU commission, stated: "As it is the leading emitter of greenhouse gases, the United States needs to take tough domestic measures. . . . [The United States] is going to try and buy its way out of its Kyoto commitments, and we are determined to prevent that from happening."[59] The quantity constraint of 50 percent domestic reductions will inflate the costs of hitting the target. As one analyst noted, "The burdens of global leadership are some-times heavy, indeed."[60]

The Origins of Technological Advance

What we choose to believe about the origins of technological advance will color the costs of the Kyoto accord. For any given target and set of policy provisions, costs decline when consumers and firms have more plentiful low-cost substitutes for high-carbon technologies. Engineering studies suggest that 20 to 25 percent of existing carbon emissions could be eliminated at low costs if people switched to new technologies like compact fluorescent light bulbs, improved thermal insulation, and energy-efficient heating and cooling systems and appliances. Engineers argue that the origins of technological advance are firmly rooted in nonprice responses—people do the right thing for the right reason. And once they understand the potential benefits of low-carbon technologies, they will just switch.

Economists disagree. They see the origins of technological advance as driven by changes in relative price. Even if new technologies are available, people do not switch unless prices induce them to switch. They are unwilling to experiment with new devices at current prices. People behave as if their time horizons are short, perhaps reflecting their uncertainty about future energy prices and the reliability of the technology. Factors other than energy efficiency—for example, quality and features and the time and effort required to learn about a new technology and how it works—also matter to consumers.

The difference in views on the origin of technological change is apparent in the debate about the autonomous rate of improvement in the energy-to-GDP ratio underlying all models of climate economics. Modelers debate the appro-priate rate of "autonomous energy efficiency improvement," the approximation of the rate of change in the energy-GDP ratio when energy prices remain relatively flat. Although historical evidence suggests that the autonomous change is about .5 percent per year, some people argue that the announcement of the Kyoto protocol will prompt businesses to accelerate the implementation of energy-efficient methods of production. That "announcement effect" has been argued to increase the autonomous rate to 2 percent per year or more. Those significant leaps are hard to justify, however, after examining the evidence. The Climate Change Action Plan has thus far spent $.5 billion to reduce carbon emissions in the United States by about 14 million metric tons. Given that we have to reduce emissions by over 500 million metric tons, we would have to believe that we are on the cusp of a very steep S-shape diffusion curve.[61]

Economists remain wary of claims that alternative energy-saving technologies are readily available at no extra cost to consumers. People do not always take advantage of cost-effective, energy-efficient technologies that, in the long run, are good for both the pocketbook and the environment. At current prices, many consumers may not be willing to experiment with compact fluorescent light bulbs, improved thermal insulation, better heating and cooling systems, and energy-efficient appliances. Several studies have estimated that when consumers buy air conditioners, space heaters, water heaters, and refrigerators, the payoff predicted by the engineers does not come through.[62] In addition, consumers' implicit time horizon can be much shorter than the time horizon reflected in market interest rates. Even when consumers are presented with estimates of the likely future cost savings, they pay more attention to immediate outlays. As our experience with the oil shocks of the 1970s shows, choices do change when prices rise. Economists contend that the most effective way to curb excessive energy consumption is to raise the price of energy to reflect the harmful effects on the environment of burning fossil fuels.

But at the White House conference on climate change in October 1998, President Clinton made it clear that he did not believe that Americans would tolerate higher energy taxes to combat climate change.[63] His answer was to promote new energy-efficient technologies rather than impose steep energy price increases. The president's plan is to allocate $6 billion for research subsidies and tax credits over five years. The Congressional Budget Office estimated that the United States currently spends nearly $5 billion annually on programs directly or indirectly related to climate protection. The CBO also concluded that the effect of current programs and tax policies "on total emissions was unclear . . . [but] it would probably be small. . . . Since most of the funds are spent to learn more about [climate change] and to improve energy efficiency in the future, the short-term effect is minimal."[64]

The theory of nonprice policy response to technology adoption must recognize that preferences can prevent adoption to the levels predicted by engineering studies. High adoption rates will be realized once prices go high enough to eliminate the barrier. For example, high carbon prices can provide the stimulus for some technologies to clear the barrier. Second, policies could be designed to try to eliminate barriers, but firms have found that those technologies are not cost-effective. Subsidies that increase their adoption will generate benefits less than the policies' costs.

Although economists do not see the average person switching energy sources just for the sake of switching, they do accept that the search for profits can create R&D breakthroughs that reduce the costs of backstop technologies.[65] Those breakthroughs change the relative prices that can induce energy users to switch from fossil fuels to solar energy. On the basis of a Hotelling model of scarcity rents, for example, Chakravorty et al. show that if historical rates of cost reduction in the production of solar energy are maintained— 30 to 50 percent per decade—more than 90 percent of the world's coal will never be used.[66] The world will make the transition to the backstop technology: to solar power from coal and oil even without a carbon tax. Global temperatures will increase by 1.5 to 2 degrees Celsius by around 2050 and will then decline steadily to preindustrial levels.

Finally, what we choose to believe about technology depends on how we think about the interaction of the technologies of risk reduction. Climate change discussions usually separate human responses to potential threats into two broad categories—mitigation and adaptation. By mitigating, humans reduce the *odds* that a bad event happens; by adapting, they reduce the *consequences* when a bad event actually does occur. But for the most part, the climate change literature has modeled mitigation and adaptation separately. That is unfortunate because significant interactions are likely to exist between how people choose to mitigate and adapt. Those risk-reduction strategies probably complement or negate each other. Understanding the interaction between the two can help formulate what we think of the Kyoto protocol. The benefits of mitigation will be lower, the more people can adapt to the climate.

People can privately and collectively affect the threats they confront. That realization may have profound impacts on the formal evaluation of climate change policy. First, researchers need to rethink the traditional risk assessment–risk management bifurcation currently applied to the research and management of climate change risk. Second, we should also acknowledge that both private and collective risk-reduction actions be considered in benefit-cost analysis and program evaluations to avoid the undervaluation of risk reductions. Third, researchers should consider the implications of when a person passes along a risk to someone else across time and space.

6

A Choice of Vision

A moderate "broad, then deep" approach with gradual emission reductions made sense before the Kyoto protocol, and it still makes sense today.[67] The accord provides no additional benefits for the extra cost it will impose relative to that alternative benchmark. We might claim that the additional cost is the price of building international trust and securing a politically credible "first step." That might well be the case. But it is not obvious to everyone that that step would not have occurred anyway or that the billions of redirected dollars could not be spent more usefully on a dozen other environmental, health, or safety issues.

But whether we believe that that matters depends on what Thomas Sowell calls our choice of vision. People with an unconstrained vision believe that we all have a vast untapped morality buried within waiting to emerge with the right direction. Thus, solutions like the Kyoto protocol are primary; the trade-offs involved are secondary. As Sowell puts it, "[E]very closer approximation to the ideal should be preferred. Costs are regrettable, but by no means decisive."[68] People with a constrained vision, however, weigh ideals against the costs of achieving them. Real incentives will be needed to get people to take on the goals of the Kyoto protocol intentionally.

The concrete message from economics is that the catastrophes have to be exceedingly probable for the protocol to make sense. But for now and the foreseeable future, the uncertainties of climate change leave enough latitude so that whether we choose to believe that the benefits justify the costs of the protocol rests on our choice of vision.

Where to now? If climate change is really just about the developed world's picking up the tab for benefits accruing to future generations in the developing world, there must be a better way—a more direct way—to do that than the Kyoto protocol. But if climate change is about more than that, we need to consider questions to forge a larger middle ground on benefits and costs. We must find the price to induce the developing countries to adopt the protocol. We must define the odds for catastrophe and surprise concepts. We must quickly examine the nature of sinks to sort out whether the costs of measurement, verification, and enforcement exceed the benefits, thereby reducing the odds that the discussion degenerates into a sideshow distraction. We must commission test studies on emission markets because effective institutional design requires no less. That approach worked for spectrum markets, and it can work for emission markets as well. We must construct real case studies to understand what institution-building exercises work across developed and developing nations. We must carefully evaluate the trade-off frontier of flexibility and stringency within political constraints. We must give more consideration to the incentives for technological progress created by different climate policies over the long term, including the opportunity cost of inducing innovation in climate protection versus other deserving goals. Finally, we must be vigilant that we are not only talking to ourselves as we sharpen the benefit and cost estimates as events unfold and new research results come forth.

Notes

1. B. Bolin, "The Kyoto Negotiations on Climate Change: A Science Perspective," *Science* 279 (January 16, 1998): 330–31

2. J. Dales, *Pollution, Property, and Prices* (Toronto: University of Toronto Press, 1968).

3. Several technical reviews of the costs and benefits of climate change policy exist. See the Intergovernment Panel on Climate Change (IPCC) Working Group III, *Climate Change 1995: Economics and Social Dimensions of Climate Change—The Contribution of Working Group III to the Second Assessment Report of the Intergovernment Panel on Climate Change*, ed. J. Bruce, H. Lee, and E. Haites (Cambridge: Cambridge University Press, 1996); and its critique, W. Nordhaus, ed., *Economics and Policy Issues in Climate Change* (Washington, D.C.: Resources for the Future, 1998). Others question whether benefit-cost analysis is useful at all considering the uncertainties involved. See, for example, the articles by B. Bolin and T. Tietenberg in the climate change policy forum in *Environmental and Development Economics* 3 (1998): 347–409.

4. See, for example, H. Jacoby, R. Prinn, and R. Schmalensee, "Kyoto's Unfinished Business," *Foreign Affairs* (July/August 1998): 54–66.

5. See R. Sedjo, B. Sohngen, and P. Jagger, *Carbon Sinks in a Post-Kyoto World*, Climate Issues Brief No. 12 (Washington, D.C.: Resources for the Future, October 1998).

6. U.S. Department of State, *The Kyoto Protocol on Climate Change: State Department Fact Sheet* (Washington, D.C.: Government Printing Office, January 15, 1998).

7. R. Cooper, "Toward a Real Global Warming Treaty," *Foreign Affairs* (March/April 1998): 66–79.

8. Quoted in S. Huber and C. Douglass, *Two Perspectives on Global Climate Change. A Briefing Book* (St. Louis: Center for the Study of American Business, Washington University, July 1998).

9. Benefits can be more than just avoided damages if we include indirect or secondary benefits such as reduced congestion or air pollution. I address the validity of that point shortly.

10. T. Wigley, "The Kyoto Protocol: CO_2, CH_4, and Climate Implications," *Geophysical Research Letters* 25 (1998): 2285–88.

11. Those aggregate estimates also mask significant variability in impacts across regions, economic sectors, and industries.

12. W. Nordhaus, "To Slow or Not to Slow: The Economics of the Greenhouse Effects," *Economic Journal* 101 (1991): 920–37.

13. D. Pearce, "Economic Development and Climate Change," *Environment and Development Economics* 3 (1998): 389–92.

14. T. Schelling, "The Costs of Combating Global Warming," *Foreign Affairs* (November/December 1997): 8–14. See also T. Schelling, "Some Economics of Global Warming," *American Economic Review* 82 (1992): 1–14.

15. See, for instance, P. Epstein, "Climate, Ecology, and Human Health," *Consequences* 3 (1997): 3–19.

16. Moore makes the case that moderately warmer weather is more conducive to human health, such that climate change might reduce mortality rates in the United States by about 40,000 per year. See T. Moore, "Health and Amenity Effects of Global Warming," *Economic Inquiry* 36 (1998): 471–88.

17. A. Krupnick, *Climate Change, Health Risks, and Economics* [database online] [cited May 1998]; available from Weathervane, www.weathervane.rff.org.

18. See T. Crocker and J. Shogren, "Endogenous Risk and Environmental Program Evaluation," in *Environmental Program Evaluation: A Primer*, ed. G. Knaap and T. J. Kim (Urbana: University of Illinois Press, 1997), 255–69; G. Duncan, "Does Poverty Affect the Life Chances of Children?" *American Sociological Review* (forthcoming); M. Kremer, "Integrating Behavioral Choice into Epidemiological Models of AIDS," *Quarterly Journal of Economics* 111 (1996): 549–74; S. Korenman and J. Miller, "Effects of Long-Term Poverty on Physical Health of Children in the National Longitudinal Survey of Youth," photocopy, 1997.

19. G. Brown and J. Shogren, "Economics of the Endangered Species Act," *Journal of Economic Perspectives* 12 (Summer 1998): 3–20.

20. R. Costanza et al., "The Value of the World's Ecosystem Services and Natural Capital," *Nature* 387 (1997): 253–60.

21. See, for example, V. K. Smith, "Mispriced Planet," *Regulation* (Summer 1997): 16–17. On reflection, most economists would agree with M. Toman's point that the $33 trillion figure is "a serious underestimate of infinite." See *Nature* 395 (October 1, 1998): 430.

22. See A. Alexander et al., "A Method for Valuing Global Ecosystem Services," *Ecological Economics* (forthcoming).

23. D. Burtraw and M. Toman, *The Benefits of Reduced Air Pollutants in the U.S. from Greenhouse Gas Mitigation Policies*, Climate Issues Brief No. 7 (Washington, D.C.: Resources for the Future, October 1997).

24. See the PM NAAQS and Ozone NAAQS Regulatory Impact Analyses, Office of Air Quality Protection and Standards, U.S. Environmental Protection Agency [database online]; available from

http://www.epa.gov/ttncaaa1/t1ria.html.

25. S. Eizenstat, "Stick with Kyoto," *Foreign Affairs* 77 (1998): 119–21.

26. J. Allen, "El Niño's Price Tag Sets No Disaster Record," *Washington Post*, April 5, 1998.

27. E. Barron, written testimony, Committee on Environment and Public Works, U.S. Senate, July 11, 1997; E. Barron, "Climate Models: How Reliable Are Their Predictions?" *Consequences* 1 (1995): 16–27.

28. In fact, some companies are being quite aggressive. British Petroleum, the world's third largest petroleum company, has taken on emission trading and has opened a new solar manufacturing facility. See S. Percy, "Making Progress beyond Kyoto," *How Workable Is the Kyoto Protocol?* [database online] [cited March 1998] available from Weathervane, www.weathervane.rff.org.

29. The "broad, then deep" approach seems to be consistent with one side of the domestic U.S. political strategy reflected in the nonbinding Byrd-Hagel resolution, passed in the Senate 95–0, that stated that the United States should accept no climate agreement that did not demand comparable sacrifices of all participants.

30. R. Schmalensee, "Greenhouse Policy Architectures and Institutions," MIT Joint Program on the Science and Policy of Global Climate Change, Report No. 13, November 1996; S. Schneider and L. Goulder, "Achieving Carbon Dioxide Targets Cost-Effectively: What Needs to Be Done Now?" *Nature* 389 (1997): 13.

31. T. Wigley, R. Richels, and J. Edmonds, "Economic and Environmental Choices in the Stabilization of Atmospheric CO_2 Concentrations," *Nature* 379 (1996): 240–43. A. Manne and R. Richels, "On Stabilizing CO_2 Concentrations: Cost-Effective Emission Reduction Strategies," *Energy Modeling Forum* 14 (April 1997).

32. The pre-Kyoto results from the president's Interagency Analysis Team are within that range as well. An exception is that the team estimates that reducing emissions to 1990 levels by 2010 would cost 900,000 jobs in 2005 and 400,000 jobs by 2010. Also see J. Yellen, "The Economics of the Kyoto Protocol," statement before the Committee on Agriculture, Nutrition, and Forestry, U.S. Senate, March 5, 1998.

33. See also see the report by the U.S. Energy Information Administration, *Impacts of the Kyoto Protocol on U.S. Energy Markets and Economic Activity* (Washington, D.C.: Government Printing Office, October 1998). The report finds that full U.S. compliance with the Kyoto protocol could raise gasoline prices 53 percent and electric rates 86 percent by the year 2010. The report predicts a drop in U.S. GNP of about 4 percent by 2010 under the worst-case scenario.

34. See, for example, W. Nordhaus, "To Slow or Not to Slow"; M. Grubb et al., "The Costs of Limiting Fossil-Fuel CO_2 Emissions: A Survey and Analysis," *Annual Review of Energy and the Environment* 18 (1993): 397–478; *Energy*

Modeling Forum Results (Stanford: EMF, 1994); J. Edmonds et al., "Return to 1990: The Costs of Mitigating United States Carbon Emissions in the Post-2000 Period," Battelle Memorial Institute, Columbus, Ohio, October 1997; W. McKibbon and P. Wilcoxen, *A Better Way to Slow Global Climate Change* (Washington, D.C.: Brookings Institution, March 1997).

35. M. Hamilton and C. Chandler, "Cures That Involve a World of Pain," *Washington Post,* November 13, 1997.

36. D. Montgomery, "Global Impacts of a Climate Change Treaty," in *The Costs of Kyoto,* ed. J. Adler (Washington, D.C.: Competitive Enterprise Institute, 1997), 57–72.

37. S. Brown et al., "The Economic Impact of International Climate Change Policy," Australian Bureau of Agricultural and Resource Economics, 1997.

38. Those estimates are robust across different modeling runs. The Energy Modeling Forum compares a diverse group of economic models employing different methodologies. Standardizing those models by assuming common exogenous parameters yielded similar results. That suggests that the choice of method is secondary to the choice of values for population growth, per capita income, energy intensity, and technical progress.

39. W. Nordhaus and J. Boyer, "Requiem for Kyoto: An Economic Analysis of the Kyoto Protocol," Yale University, photocopy, June 29, 1998.

40. Discussions with Ray Squitieri, U.S. Department of Treasury.

41. See also R. Repetto and D. Austin, *The Costs of Climate Protection,* World Resources Institute, 1997.

42. J. Warrick, "'People Are Sweltering,' says Gore, Tying Record Heat to Global Warming," *Washington Post,* July 15, 1998.

43. S. Lichtenstein et al. "The Judged Frequency of Lethal Events," *Journal of Experimental Psychology* 4 (1978): 551–78; W. K. Viscusi, *Fatal Tradeoffs: Public and Private Responsibilities for Risk* (New York: Oxford University Press, 1992).

44. See, for example, J. Fox et al., "Consumer Preferences for Irradiation Given Alternative Information," working paper, Kansas State University, July 1998.

45. See, for example, A. Blinder, "Needed: Planet Insurance," *New York Times,* October 22, 1997.

46. The economics literature on catastrophes includes M. Cropper, "Regulating Activities with Catastrophic Environmental Consequences," *Journal of Environmental Economics and Management* 3 (1976): 1–15; H. Clarke and W. Reed, "Consumption/Pollution Trade-offs in an Environment Vulnerable to Pollution-Related Catastrophic Collapse," *Journal of Economic Dynamics and Control* 18 (1994): 991–1010; O. Eismont and H. Welsch, "Optimal Greenhouse Gas Emissions under Various Assessments of Climate Change Ambiguity," *Environmental and Resource Economics* 8 (1996): 129–40.

47. S. Peck and T. Teisberg, "Uncertainty and the Value of Information with Stochastic Losses from Global Warming," *Risk Analysis* 16 (1996): 227–35.

48. W. Nordhaus, "Expert Opinion on Climatic Change," *American Scientist* (1994): 45–51.

49. T. Roughgarden, "Quantifying the Damage of Climate Change: Implications for the DICE Model," Stanford University, March 14, 1997.

50. J. Gjerde, S. Grepperud, and S. Kverndokk, *Optimal Climate Policy under the Possibility of a Catastrophe*, Statistics Norway, February 1998.

51. D. Kelly and C. Kolstad, "Bayesian Learning and Accumulation of Stock Externalities," University of California-Santa Barbara, 1996.

52. One guess is that carbon leakage would probably be between 10 and 50 percent. See T. Rutherford, "International Competitiveness and National Plans," University of Colorado, 1995.

53. See the recent ideas by R. Hahn and R. Stavins, "Thoughts on Designing an International Greenhouse Gas Trading System," John F. Kennedy School of Government, Harvard University, September 1998.

54. See J. Shogren, "Lessons from the Lab," *Regulation* (Fall 1997): 5–6.

55. See, for example, R. Stavins, "The Costs of Carbon Sequestration: A Revealed-Preference Approach," *American Economic Review* (forthcoming).

56. Discussion with Brent Sohngen, Ohio State University, August 1998.

57. H. Jacoby, R. Prinn, and R. Schmalensee, "Kyoto's Unfinished Business," *Foreign Affairs* (July/August 1998): 54–66.

58. I. W. H. Parry, "Reducing Carbon Emissions: Interactions with the Tax System Raise Costs," *Resources* 128 (Summer 1997): 9–12.

59. "Europe Union Starts Planning Strategy to Stress Domestic Action under Kyoto Pact," *Daily Environment Report* 1060-2976/98, March 31, 1998.

60. J. Firor, "U.S. Needs to Lead by Example in Reducing Emissions," in *How Workable Is the Kyoto Protocol?* [database online] [cited March 1998]; available from Weathervane, www.weathervane.rff.org.

61. *United States Climate Action Report—1997*, U.S. Department of State (Washington, D.C.: Government Printing Office, July 1997).

62. See, for example, G. Metcalf and K. Hassett, "Measuring the Energy Savings from Home Improvements Investments: Evidence from Monthly Billing Data," NBER working paper 6074, June 1997.

63. "Clinton Opposes Higher Energy Taxes to Curb Global Warming," *New York Times*, October 7, 1997.

64. Congressional Budget Office, *Climate Change: The Policy Challenge and Current Programs* (Washington, D.C.: Government Printing Office, August 1998).

65. L. Goulder and S. Schneider, "Induced Technological Change and the Attractiveness of CO_2 Abatement Policies," *Resource and Energy Economics* (forthcoming).

66. U. Chakravorty, J. Roumasset, and K. Tse, "Endogenous Substitution among Energy Resources and Global Warming," *Journal of Political Economy* 105 (1997): 1201–34.

67. Hahn suggests that a better first step would be a series of institution-building exercises aimed at engaging developing nations in climate change policy. R. Hahn, *The Economics and Politics of Climate Change* (Washington, D.C.: AEI Press, 1998). That approach could make sense, especially if one addresses the historical fact that once a problem is transformed into institutional rules, interest groups that invested in those rules will fight to keep them, regardless of the inefficiency. See B. Yandle, "Bootleggers, Baptists, and Global Warming," PERC Policy Series PS-14, November 1998.

68. T. Sowell, *A Conflict of Visions: Ideological Origins of Political Struggles* (New York: William Morrow, 1987), 34.

About the Author

JASON SHOGREN is the Stroock Distinguished Professor of Natural Resource Conservation and Management and professor of economics at the University of Wyoming. Previously, he taught at Appalachian State University, Iowa State University, and Yale University. In 1997 Mr. Shogren served as the senior economist for environmental and natural resource policy on the Council of Economic Advisers. He was an associate editor of the *Journal of Environmental Economics and Management* and is currently an associate editor of the *American Journal of Agricultural Economics*. He is the coauthor of *Environmental Economics in Theory and Practice* (Oxford University Press, 1996) and editor of *Private Property and the Endangered Species Act: Saving Habitats, Protecting Homes* (University of Texas Press, 1999). He has published numerous essays on risk, conflict, valuation, environmental policy, and experimental economics.

AEI STUDIES ON GLOBAL ENVIRONMENTAL POLICY
Robert W. Hahn, Series Editor

THE BENEFITS AND COSTS OF THE KYOTO PROTOCOL
Jason Shogren

COSTS AND BENEFITS OF GREENHOUSE GAS REDUCTION
Thomas C. Schelling

THE ECONOMICS AND POLITICS OF CLIMATE CHANGE
Robert W. Hahn

THE GREENING OF GLOBAL WARMING
Robert Mendelsohn

MAKING ENVIRONMENTAL POLICY: TWO VIEWS
Irwin M. Stelzer and Paul R. Portney

WHAT HAS THE KYOTO PROTOCOL WROUGHT?
Robert W. Hahn and Robert N. Stavins

WHY SOVEREIGNTY MATTERS
Jeremy Rabkin